James Taylor

A RETROSPECTIVE

James Taylor

A RETROSPECTIVE

CONTENTS

Cover photography by **PETER SIMON/LYNN GOLDSMITH INC.**
Designed by **KOSH & CO**

James Taylor

MUD SLIDE SLIM

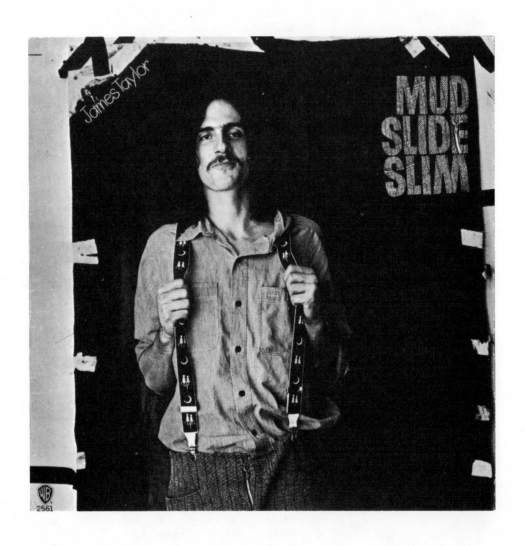

MUD SLIDE SLIM

Words and Music by
JAMES TAYLOR

LOVE HAS BROUGHT ME AROUND

Words and Music by
JAMES TAYLOR

13

Love has brought_me a-round._ Love has brought_me a-round,_ yes, it has._

Love has brought_me a-round._ Love has brought_me a-round._

When my _ Now I know you _ know

what I've got_ to say is an old cli-ché_

PLACES IN MY PAST

Words and Music by
JAMES TAYLOR

RIDING ON A RAILROAD

Words and Music by
JAMES TAYLOR

SOLDIERS

Words and Music by
JAMES TAYLOR

26

YOU CAN CLOSE YOUR EYES

Words and Music by
JAMES TAYLOR

this old world must still be spin-nin' 'round.
no one's gon - na take that time a - way.
And

I still love you.
You can stay as long as you like.
So

close your eyes.
You can close your eyes, it's all right.

I don't know no love songs,
and

HEY MISTER, THAT'S ME UP ON THE JUKEBOX

Words and Music by
JAMES TAYLOR

LET ME RIDE

Words and Music by
JAMES TAYLOR

HIGHWAY SONG

Words and Music by
JAMES TAYLOR

ISN'T IT NICE TO BE HOME AGAIN

Words and Music by
JAMES TAYLOR

Late last night, so far a-way, I dreamed my-self a dream.

Well, I dreamed I was so all a-lone.

Is-n't it nice to be home a-gain? I said,

LONG AGO AND FAR AWAY

Words and Music by
JAMES TAYLOR

50

James Taylor

WALKING MAN

WALKING MAN

Words and Music by
JAMES TAYLOR

Vocal Ad Lib

He's the walking man, born to walk,
Walk on, walking man.
Well now, would he have wings to fly,
Would he be free?
Golden wings against the sky.
Walking man, walk on by,
So long, walking man, so long.

ME AND MY GUITAR

Words and Music by
JAMES TAYLOR

Vocal Ad Lib

Oh, maybe a few friends fall by for tea,
A little bit of who do you love.
But pay no attention to the man behind the curtain,
It's me and my guitar.
Having fun, boogie, woogie, uh-huh,
Me and my guitar.

ROCK 'N' ROLL IS MUSIC NOW

Words and Music by
JAMES TAYLOR

Ma - ma knows and pa - pa knows that rock 'n' roll is mu - sic,
Ten - nis shoes and rhy-thm and blues are sec - ond gen - er - a - tion

rock 'n' roll is mu - sic now. ___
all a - cross the na - tion now. ___

LET IT ALL FALL DOWN

Words and Music by
JAMES TAYLOR

DADDY'S BABY

Words and Music by
JAMES TAYLOR

HELLO OLD FRIEND

Words and Music by
JAMES TAYLOR

FADING AWAY

Words and Music by
JAMES TAYLOR

MIGRATION

Words and Music by
JAMES TAYLOR

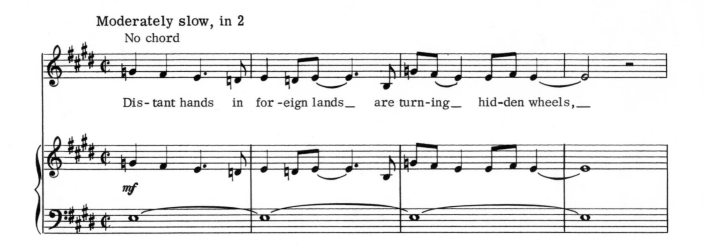

Moderately slow, in 2

No chord

Dis-tant hands in for-eign lands__ are turn-ing__ hid-den wheels,__

caus-ing things to come a-bout__ which no one seems to feel. All in-

D/E   A/E   Asus4/E   E

vis-i-ble from where we stand,__ the con-nec-tions come to pass, and

James Taylor

GORILLA

MUSIC

Words and Music by
JAMES TAYLOR

98

WANDERING

Traditional—Musical Adaptation and Additional Lyrics by
JAMES TAYLOR

I've been wan - d'rin' ear - ly and late, ___ from
been in the ar - my, I've worked on a farm, ___ and
Snakes in the o - cean, eels ___ in the sea, ___ I let a

New York Cit - y to the Gold - en ___ Gate. }
all I've got to show is the mus - cle in my arm. } And it
red - head - ed wom - an make a fool out of me. }

102

GORILLA

Words and Music by
JAMES TAYLOR

104

MEXICO

Words and Music by
JAMES TAYLOR

YOU MAKE IT EASY

Words and Music by
JAMES TAYLOR

111

LIGHTHOUSE

Words and Music by
JAMES TAYLOR

114

115

Off the coast of Af - ri - ca,__ bound for South A - mer - i - ca,__ a

world a-way from here,__ is a ship that sails__ the sea,__

is a man who's just__ like me_ and I wish that I_ was there.__

Repeat and fade (vocal ad lib)

Repeat and fade

I WAS A FOOL TO CARE

Words and Music by
JAMES TAYLOR

Moderately slow, in 2

ANGRY BLUES

Words and Music by
JAMES TAYLOR

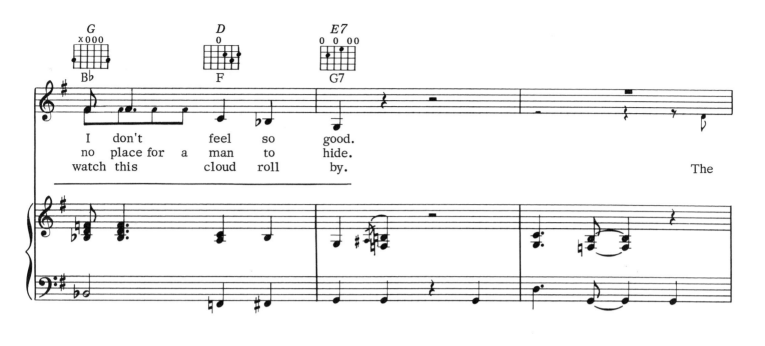

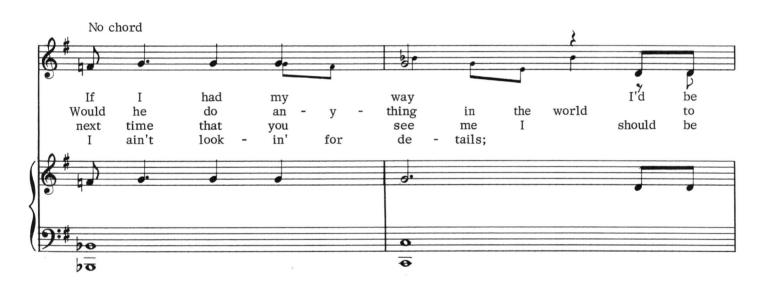

LOVE SONGS

Words and Music by
JAMES TAYLOR

SARAH MARIA

Words and Music by
JAMES TAYLOR

136

James Taylor

IN THE POCKET

SHOWER THE PEOPLE

Words and Music by
JAMES TAYLOR

Shower The People - 2

Vocal Ad Lib

They say in every life,
They say the rain must fall.
Just like a pouring rain,
Make it rain.
Love is sunshine.

A JUNKIE'S LAMENT

Words and Music by
JAMES TAYLOR

MONEY MACHINE

Words and Music by
JAMES TAYLOR

bring your en - e - mies __ to their knees, __ with the pos - si - ble ex - cep-tion of the

North Vi - et - nam-ese. It takes a strong hit from the

mon-ey ma-chine, __ sit-tin' on top, on top of the world.

Strong hit from the mon-ey ma-chine, __ sit-tin' on top, on

EVERYBODY HAS THE BLUES

Words and Music by
JAMES TAYLOR

DADDY'S ALL GONE

Words and Music by
JAMES TAYLOR

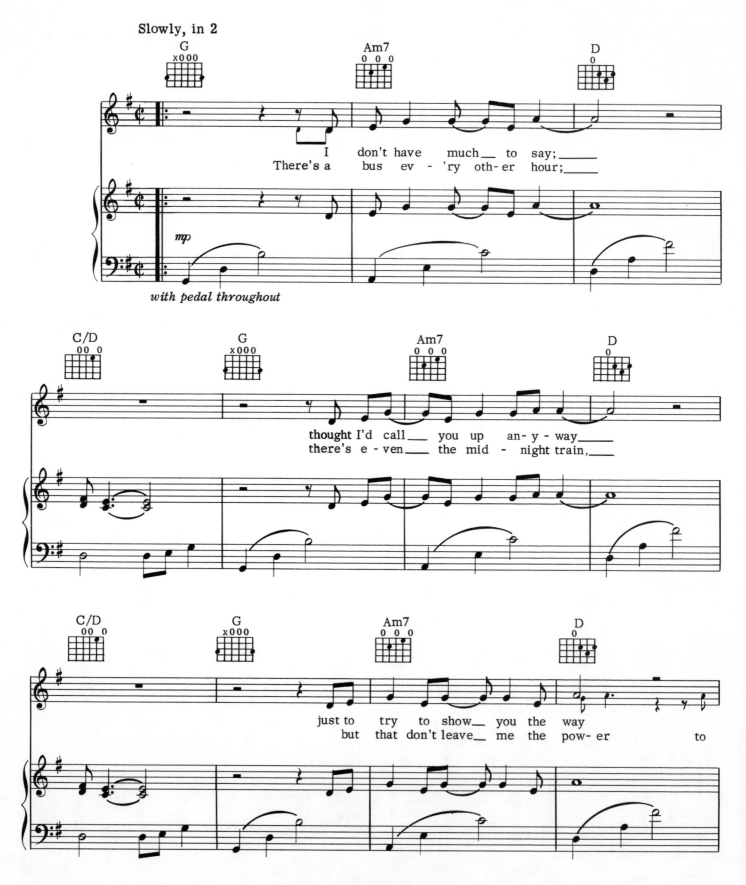

say-ing please _____ don't__ let ____ the show__ go
say-ing please _____ don't__ make ____ the show__ go

on.
on.

SLOW BURNING LOVE

Words and Music by
JAMES TAYLOR

164

CAPTAIN JIM'S DRUNKEN DREAM

Words and Music by
JAMES TAYLOR

Now, you coun - try fools__ in your one - horse town,__ you can
see me com - in', you wink__ your eye and call me
know that the Yan - kee whis - key is

laugh at me.__
Cap - tain Jim.__
tak - in' a - way my mind

It's plain as rain__ that you've
And when I don't do noth - in' but to
and I know that rum__ is the

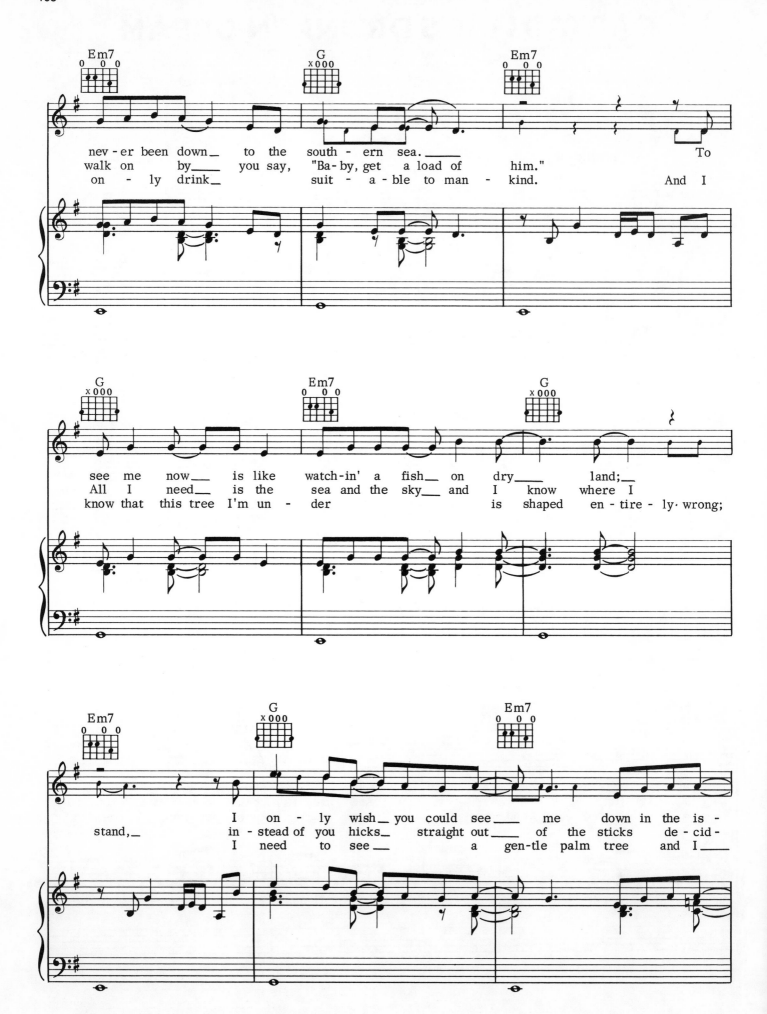

NOTHING LIKE A HUNDRED MILES

Words and Music by
JAMES TAYLOR

Moderately fast

I have tried _____ to for-get a-bout you; ___

ba - by, I have failed.__ Just as long as I

stay___ in Hous - ton I will.____

FAMILY MAN

Words and Music by
JAMES TAYLOR

180

Vocal Ad Lib

If I can ever lose my blues
Walk on over and turn on the TV
What I'd like to do is lie down on the sofa
Later on
I might walk my dog
Bo Diddley's a family man

GOLDEN MOMENTS

Words and Music by
JAMES TAYLOR

James Taylor

JT

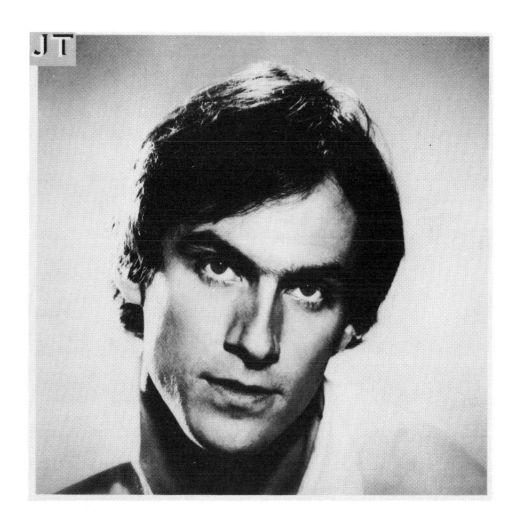

YOUR SMILING FACE

Words and Music by
JAMES TAYLOR

188

Tell me how _ much long - er; it will grow strong-er ev - 'ry day. _

Oh, _ how much long - er? I

thought I was in love a cou-ple of times _ be - fore _____ with the girl _ next door. _

_ But that was long _ be-fore I met _ you. Now, I'm sure _ that I won't for-get _

* Move capo to 4th fret.

189

* Move capo to 6th fret.

LOOKING FOR LOVE ON BROADWAY

Words and Music by
JAMES TAYLOR

THERE WE ARE

Words and Music by
JAMES TAYLOR

198

you, but you hold my heart in your hand.

And I found out some-thing a-bout you: ba - by, with-out

you, I'm a lone-ly man.

D.C. al Coda

So

Coda

ANOTHER GREY MORNING

Words and Music by
JAMES TAYLOR

BARTENDER'S BLUES

Words and Music by
JAMES TAYLOR

folks with their_ backs_ to the wall.
pack up and_ mail_ in my key.
strand-ed at the edge_ of the sea.
But I need four walls_ a-

round me _____ to hold my life;_ to keep me_ from_ go-ing_a-stray;_

and a hon-ky-tonk an-gel _____ to hold me tight_ to keep me_ from_

1. 2.
slip-ping_____ a-way.

I can
Now, the slip-ping_ a-way.

3.

SECRET O' LIFE

Words and Music by
JAMES TAYLOR

I WAS ONLY TELLING A LIE

Words and Music by
JAMES TAYLOR

TRAFFIC JAM

Words and Music by
JAMES TAYLOR

TERRA NOVA

Words and Music by
JAMES TAYLOR and CARLY SIMON

220

223

224

IF I KEEP MY HEART OUT OF SIGHT

Words and Music by
JAMES TAYLOR

James Taylor

FLAG

COMPANY MAN

Words and Music by
JAMES TAYLOR

JOHNNIE COMES BACK

Words and Music by
JAMES TAYLOR

I WILL NOT LIE FOR YOU

Words and Music by
JAMES TAYLOR

BROTHER TRUCKER

Words and Music by
JAMES TAYLOR

246

IS THAT THE WAY YOU LOOK?

Words and Music by
JAMES TAYLOR

B.S.U.R.

Words and Music by
JAMES TAYLOR

258

MILLWORKER

Words and Music by
JAMES TAYLOR

Moderately, in 2

Now, my grand-fa-ther was a sail - or. He
Mill-work ain't eas - y;

blew in off — the wa - ter. My fa-ther was a farm-
mill-work ain't ___ hard. ___ Mill-work, it ain't noth-

er, and I, ___ his on - ly daugh - ter, ___ I'm
ing but an aw-ful bor - ing job. ___

* Guitarists: Tune 6th string down to D.

CHANSON FRANÇAISE

Words and Music by
JAMES TAYLOR

268

SLEEP COME FREE ME

Words and Music by
JAMES TAYLOR

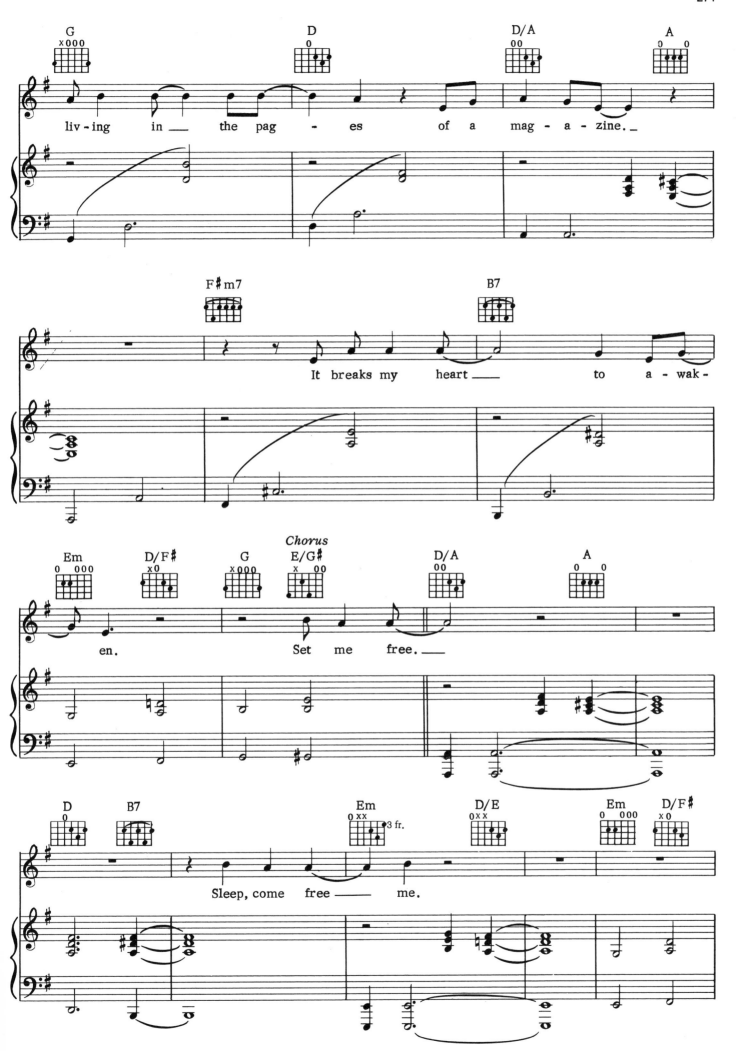

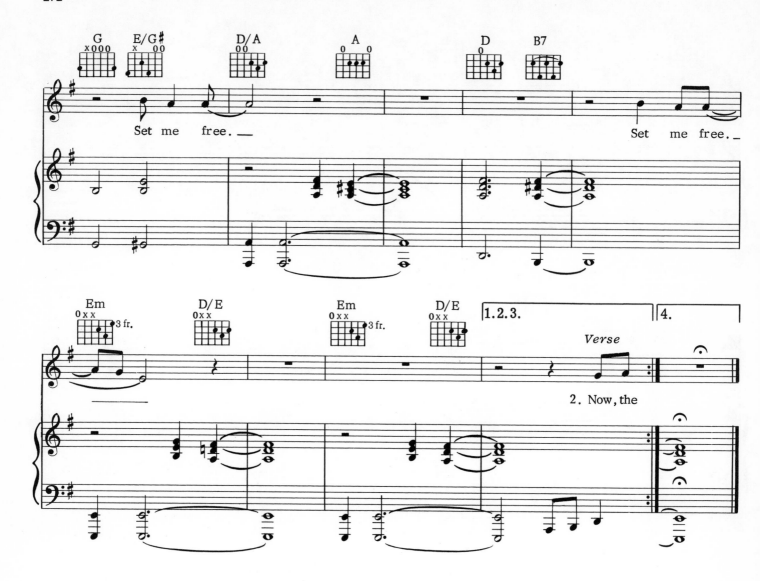

Set me free. ___

Set me free. ___

2. Now, the

2. Now, the state of Alabama says I killed a man.
The jury reached the same conclusion.
I remember I was there with a tire iron in my hand.
The rest is all confusion.

(Chorus)

3. More like an animal and less like a man,
What they leave you ain't worth keeping.
Brother, let me tell you, I got a clock with no hands.
The only way out is through sleeping.

(Chorus)

4. You get to where you used to be, whoever you claim.
It's open to interpretation.
Just remember your number and abandon your name.
And hold on to your imagination.

(Chorus)